SCIENCE FILES

GLASS

Please visit our web site at: www.garethstevens.com
For a free color catalog describing Gareth Stevens Publishing's
list of high-quality books and multimedia programs,
call 1-800-542-2595 or fax your request to (414) 332-3567.

Library of Congress Cataloging-in-Publication Data

Parker, Steve.
    Glass / by Steve Parker. — North American ed.
      p. cm. — (Science files. Materials)
    Includes bibliographical references and index.
    Summary: Discusses the unusual nature of glass, how it is made, and the many uses
to which it has been put, from fine art to industrial applications, throughout history.
    ISBN 0-8368-3082-2 (lib. bdg.)
    1. Glass—Juvenile literature. [1. Glass.] I. Title.
TP857.3.P37   2002
666'.1—dc21   2001054232

This North American edition first published in 2002 by
Gareth Stevens Publishing
A World Almanac Education Group Company
330 West Olive Street, Suite 100
Milwaukee, WI 53212 USA

Original edition © 2001 by David West Children's Books. First published in Great Britain
in 2001 by Heinemann Library, Halley Court, Jordan Hill, Oxford OX2 8EJ, a division of Reed
Educational and Professional Publishing Limited. This U.S. edition © 2002 by Gareth Stevens, Inc.
Additional end matter © 2002 by Gareth Stevens, Inc.

David West Editor: James Pickering
David West Designers: Rob Shone, Fiona Thorne, David West
Picture Research: Carrie Haines
Gareth Stevens Editor: Alan Wachtel
Gareth Stevens Designer and Cover Design: Katherine A. Goedheer

Photo Credits:
Abbreviations: (t) top, (m) middle, (b) bottom, (l) left, (r) right

The Art Archive: Museo Civico Udine/Dagli Orti (7br); Eileen Tweedy (Cover [m], 9tl, 17b).
Mary Evans Picture Library: 15b, 28bl, 28br; Paul Keevil (23m).
Glass Manufacturing Federation: 14m, 24t.
Glassworks, Hampton: 14-15b.
Robert Harding Picture Library: Bildagentur Schuster/Bramaz (Cover [tr], 28-29); M.H. Black (16b);
Martyn F. Chillmaid (7b, 22t); Lee Frost (3, 19b); Esben Hardt (25br); Hartmann/Sachs/Phototake,
NYC (27b); Raj Kamal (20t); Adam Woolfitt (11t); tr, 8, 12t, 14l, 14r, 16mr, 23t, 25l.
Waltraud Krase/D.G. Bank, Berlin: 4-5, 16t.
Ann Ronan Picture Library: 5t, 10ml, 11m.
Science Photo Library: 29b; Tony Craddock (6l); Mehau Kulyk (20m); Frank Morgan (13tl); David
Parker (26t, 26-27t); Philippe Plailly (5b); Rosenfeld Images Ltd. (10mr, 11mr); Victor de Schwanberg
(4t, 13m); Maximilian Stock Ltd. (29t); Geoff Tompkinson (21t, 22b); Ed Young (26b).
Spectrum Color Library: 8b, 13br.

Printed in the United States of America

1 2 3 4 5 6 7 8 9 06 05 04 03 02

SCIENCE FILES

materials

GLASS

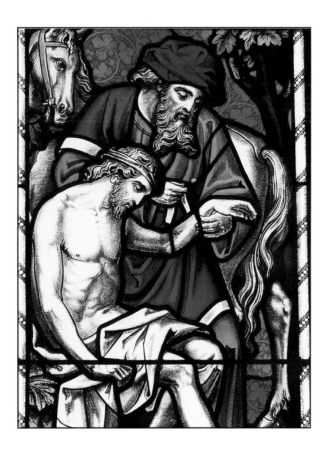

Steve Parker

Gareth Stevens Publishing
A WORLD ALMANAC EDUCATION GROUP COMPANY

CONTENTS

Factories make lots of glass bottles each day. These bottles are easy to recycle.

INTRODUCTION

Glass, one of the world's most important and useful materials, is something we hardly even see. It is specially designed to be invisible. Glass protects our homes from the wind, rain, and cold and allows us to see our drinks in their containers. Glass is hardly ever noticed, but it's all around us. We use it every day, and it's an easy material to recycle. Glass is very hi-tech, too. Special types of glass are used in computers, lasers, eyeglasses, cameras, electronic machines, light bulbs, and bright, sparkling decorations. A world without glass would be dark and dull!

This engraving shows glassmaking, one of the oldest crafts. People have shaped and colored glass by hand for thousands of years.

Glass is beautiful. Amazing glass "clouds" hang in the hall of DG Bank, Berlin, Germany.

Incredibly thin, long, flexible rods of glass carry flashes of laser light in fiberoptic telephone cables.

WHAT IS GLASS?

Glass is very difficult to describe. One technical way of describing it is as a "supercooled liquid." This means that when heated above a certain temperature, it is a clear, colorless liquid, like water. When it cools down to a normal temperature, it becomes hard and stiff. It still has many features of a liquid, rather than a solid, but it cannot run or flow anymore. Glass is like a hard liquid!

This glass building is at Futuroscope, Poitiers, France. Its shape is based on the crystals in sand that are important minerals in making glass.

LIQUID OR SOLID?

Another technical name for glass is an "amorphous solid." Looked at under a microscope, most hard, stiff substances are seen to be made up of tiny parts, such as crystals. Glass is not. It has no particular tiny shapes or structures inside.

MAKING GLASS

The most important raw material for making glass is sand. Sand contains the mineral silica, which is made of the elements silicon and oxygen, as silicon dioxide (SiO_2). Silica is heated with other minerals, including limestone (calcium carbonate) and soda ash (sodium carbonate). The mixture is melted and is then cooled quickly to form glass.

Sand (top) and limestone (above) are important raw materials for making most types of glass. They are dug from huge quarries and stored, ready for use.

FACTS FROM THE PAST

About 6,000 years ago glass was used as a hard, shiny covering, or glaze, on beads. Early glass jars and bowls were made in molds about 3,500 years ago.

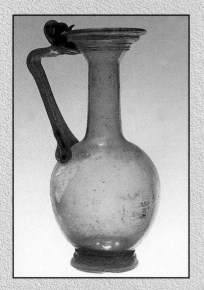

A 2,000-year-old glass pitcher

7

GLASSBLOWING

When air is blown into a liquid, it forms a bubble. Glass heated to more than about 1,830° Fahrenheit (1,000° Celsius) becomes a liquid — molten glass. If you blow into it through a long pipe, a bubble forms inside. With practice, you can form the molten glass into a beautiful goblet, vase, or cup.

AGE-OLD CRAFT

The craft of glassblowing has changed very little for almost 2,000 years. A long metal tube, the blowpipe, is dipped into a container of very hot, molten glass. The blowpipe is twirled around to collect a blob of glass on its end, as syrup is gathered on a spoon.

The glassblower may reheat the glass (right) to keep it soft while it is blown and shaped into items such as wineglasses (left).

8

The ship in this 19th-century blown-glass bottle was inserted with its masts flat.

BLOWING A BUBBLE

The glassblower puffs down the blowpipe to push air into the blob of molten glass, which expands like a balloon. Twisting the blowpipe keeps the growing "bubble" of glass, called the parison, smooth and round. The glassblower may hold it against various surfaces or place it in a hollow mold to shape it. Gradually the glass is blown, twisted, and pressed. As it cools, it hardens into its final shape.

IDEAS FOR THE FUTURE

Imagine a glass bubble so big that it covered a city! This could not happen here on Earth. Our planet's gravity gives glass weight, which would make a giant glass bubble sag and crack. In space, however, there is no gravity. Glass could be blown into a huge dome, which might then be used to cover a settlement on the Moon.

Glass — keeps air in and space out?

TOOLS AND TECHNIQUES

Each stage of glassblowing has its special tools and techniques. The blob of molten glass collected on the end of the blowpipe is called the gather. It is rolled on a smooth metal slab to make the parison. The glassblower keeps the bubble of glass twirling to make sure it stays smooth and round. Extra pieces of glass, such as the handle of a jug or the stem of a wineglass, can be added while the glass is still very hot, soft, and sticky.

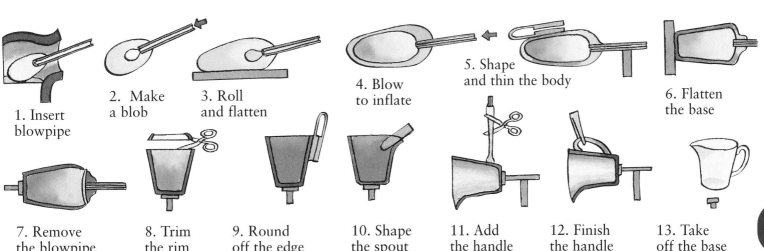

1. Insert blowpipe
2. Make a blob
3. Roll and flatten
4. Blow to inflate
5. Shape and thin the body
6. Flatten the base
7. Remove the blowpipe
8. Trim the rim
9. Round off the edge
10. Shape the spout
11. Add the handle
12. Finish the handle
13. Take off the base

FLOAT GLASS

When oil floats on water, it spreads out into a thin, flat layer. Glass sheets are made thin and flat by floating molten glass on tin.

CROWNS AND CYLINDERS

Sheets of glass were once made in two ways. In the crown method, a blob of glass was spun around so it flattened into a wide disk. In the cylinder method, a glass blob was blown into the shape of a cylinder, which was cut and flattened.

Glass panels on some skyscapers gleam like mirrors.

FLOAT GLASS

1. Raw materials: silica, lime, soda ash, cullet, and extra minerals rich in calcium, magnesium, and aluminum

Raw materials melt in the furnace.

Workers check the process.

2. Melting furnace

3. Glass floats on molten tin

4. Controlled cooling

2,730° F

2,010° F   Molten tin   1,110° F

1,020° F   390° F

The raw materials for float glass are heated to 2,730° F (1,500° C) to form a runny, molten mass. In a special airtight chamber, the molten glass spreads over the perfectly smooth surface of molten tin. It cools slowly as it is moved into a cooling chamber.

A NEW INVENTION

In the 1950s, Pilkington glassmakers invented a faster way of making sheet glass — the float method. Compared to glass made by the old methods, the sheets are smoother, thinner, more even in thickness, and much larger. In the float glass-making process (*see below*), raw ingredients are heated to make molten glass in the usual way. The molten glass spreads out like molasses over a surface of tin, a metal that is also heated until it is molten. The molten glass floats on top of the molten tin like oil floats on water. We look through the results every day as we gaze out of windows.

Careful cooling prevents cracks.

Sheets are stored in a warehouse before delivery.

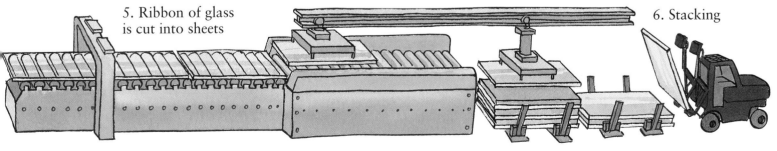

5. Ribbon of glass is cut into sheets

6. Stacking

The glass emerges from the cooling chamber, or annealing lehr, as a clear, hard ribbon, without cracks or hazy areas. The ribbon is sliced by sharp blades into separate sheets. The glass sheets are picked up by arms fitted with suction cups and taken to warehouses.

THE GLASS FACTORY

Handmade glass items are beautiful but costly. Most ordinary glass objects, such as bottles, jars, and light bulbs, are mass-produced by machines in factories.

BLOBS AND GOBS

The machine measures out a gob — a blob of molten, runny glass. The gob falls into a hollow container called the mold. The opening of the mold may be in the shape of the final item, such as a rod or ball. The molten glass flows into it, takes up this shape, and cools and hardens. The mold is then opened to release the item.

HOLLOW SHAPES

For hollow glass objects like bottles, the machine puffs a measured amount of air into the glass gob. The gob blows out and presses against the sides of the mold. In some cases, the object is fully shaped in one mold. In other cases it is first partly shaped in a blank mold. The resulting piece, called the blank, is then put into a second mold, called the blow mold, for final shaping.

To make colored light bulbs, pigments (colored substances) are mixed into the molten glass as it is made in the furnace.

STORY OF A BOTTLE

Molten glass from the furnace flows straight into the bottle-making machine. First the liquid glass gob is puffed into a bottle-like shape, called the blank. Then,

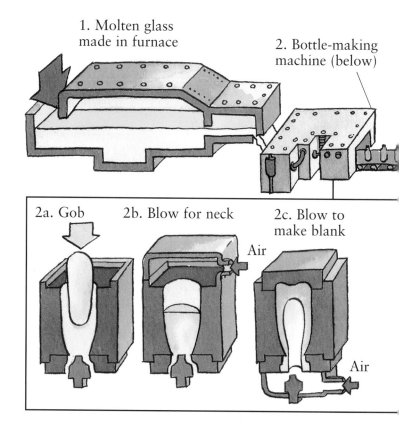

1. Molten glass made in furnace

2. Bottle-making machine (below)

2a. Gob   2b. Blow for neck   2c. Blow to make blank

Air

Air

12

TUBES AND PIPES

Glass tubes are made for many purposes. Molten glass flows through the small gap around a spinning, tapered, hollow mandrel as air blows through the mandrel. The result is a tube of soft, flexible glass, which is pulled along by grips on a conveyor belt.

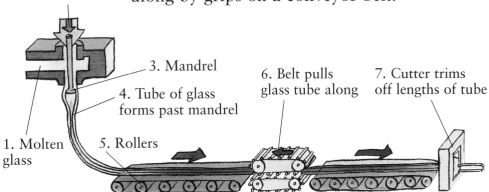

2. Air

3. Mandrel

4. Tube of glass forms past mandrel

1. Molten glass

5. Rollers

6. Belt pulls glass tube along

7. Cutter trims off lengths of tube

Manufacturing of glass tubes for fluorescent light bulbs

the blank is finished in the blow mold. The annealing lehr carefully controls the temperature of the bottles as they cool so the glass stays strong.

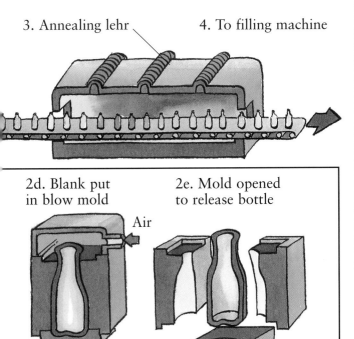

3. Annealing lehr

4. To filling machine

2d. Blank put in blow mold

Air

2e. Mold opened to release bottle

Bottle-making machines produce millions of bottles weekly. The bottles' shape comes directly from the blow mold. Some bottle shapes are known all over the world.

13

DECORATIVE GLASS

Glass windows and bottles are useful and practical. But many glass objects are not made to be used. They are produced for their beauty, shape, color, and sparkle. This kind of item is known as "decorative glass."

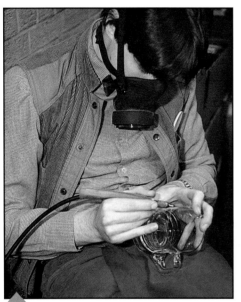 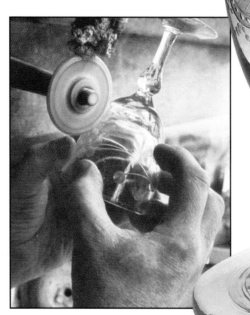

This craftsman engraves the surface of a glass using tiny drills and grinding wheels. Engraving produces delicate patterns like those on this wineglass (above).

NOT SHINY

Decorative glass is not always shiny. Its smooth surface can be cut or roughened by various methods to leave frosty-looking lines and patterns. The methods include engraving with rubbing and grinding tools, etching with chemicals such as acids, and sandblasting with high-power air bursts carrying tiny particles. Glass can also be decorated with printing, but inks tend to rub off of it.

Glass is hard, but marks can be made on it by fast-moving particles such as grains of sand. These particles remove the smooth shine and give the glass a "frosted" look. Artists use this technique to make pictures on glass doors.

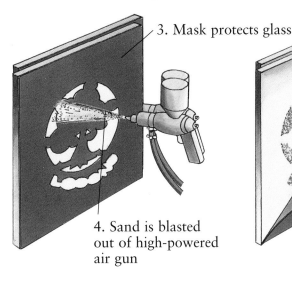

1. Thick plastic mask with design cut out

2. Mask is stuck on to glass

3. Mask protects glass

4. Sand is blasted out of high-powered air gun

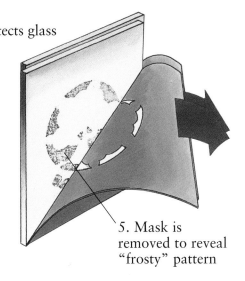

5. Mask is removed to reveal "frosty" pattern

Patterned glass is decorative, but it is not see-through, and so it can help keep a room private.

COLORED GLASS

The color of glass can be changed by painting it or covering it with plastic. But these changes only affect its surface. The glass itself can be colored all the way through as it is made *(see page 12)*, yet still remain see-through, by adding substances called pigments to the molten glass. Most pigments are made of metal-containing minerals. For example, copper-containing pigments produce red or light blue glass. Chromium pigments turn glass green, while cobalt pigments give glass a deep blue color.

FACTS FROM THE PAST

Decorative glassmaking thrived in Europe starting in the 12th century. From the 15th century, Venice, Italy, was the major center for the craft.

16th-century glassmaking

SHAPED GLASS

Mass production by machines is ideal for everyday glass objects. But special handcrafting skills are needed to shape beautiful works of art out of glass.

HOTTER AND HOTTER

When you heat a piece of glass, it softens until you can bend it with special tools. More heat makes it softer still, so you can squeeze it like modeling clay. Yet more heat turns glass into a liquid. Artists shape glass by hand by using different amounts of heat to soften the glass.

These amazing "clouds" hang in Berlin, Germany. They are among the world's largest glass objects.

Special equipment for laboratories is "custom-made" by hand.

GLASS ZOO

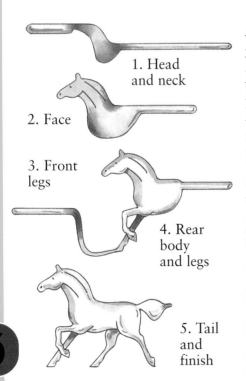

1. Head and neck

2. Face

3. Front legs

4. Rear body and legs

5. Tail and finish

Animal figures are made from several pieces of glass. A length of rod is heated in the middle so that it sags into a blob. While still hot and soft, it is shaped with tweezers and pressing tools to form the face. A thinner rod is heated so that it fuses onto the body. Then it is bent to make a leg. More pieces are added until the animal is formed.

TRICKS OF THE TRADE

The traditional methods of hand shaping glass, called lampworking, have changed little over the years. When two pieces of glass are each heated to their melting point, they can be fused together, meaning the two can be joined. A heated rod or tube can be drawn, or stretched out very thin. Glass also can be squashed much thicker. Air blown into the hollow part of the object makes it bubble out like a balloon. Dimples, or points, can be made with small spatulas, tweezers, and other tools.

Microwave melt?

IDEAS FOR THE FUTURE

Glass softens for shaping when it is very hot, usually more than 1,830° F (1,000° C). The heat usually comes from a lamp flame. One day, a new microwave oven might do the job. Glass for recycling could be melted down quickly and cheaply.

PRESSED GLASS

Pressing is a simple method of making glass items, such as cups and bowls, where the open end, or mouth, is the widest part. The gob of glass is pressed into shape between the two parts of a mold. The surface design can be very complicated.

1. Drop gob
2. Lower mold
3. Press hard
4. Open

Handmade perfume bottles from the 1930s were made in the popular art deco style.

SPECIAL GLASS

There are thousands of kinds of glass. Each has its own important features and special uses.

"COOKING" GLASS

Making different kinds of glass is like cooking. The end result depends on the mixture of ingredients, or raw materials, heated in the furnace. Adding a certain substance to the mixture can give the glass different features. For example, adding lead oxide, instead of calcium minerals, makes the glass glint, sparkle, and twinkle in the light. This is called lead crystal glass. It is used especially for engraved wineglasses.

Only a very few chemicals, such as hydrofluoric acid, can destroy glass. So glass flasks, jars, and beakers are ideal for holding dangerous substances.

Sunglasses are made with tinted glass. Reactive sunglasses can change from clear to tinted when the Sun comes out.

HOT OR COLD DRINK?

A vacuum bottle, or thermos, has many ways of insulating. The plastic case and the air gap inside it are good insulators. So is the glass of the inner container, which has two layers with a vacuum, another excellent insulator, in between. The result is that hot drinks stay hot — and cold drinks stay cold.

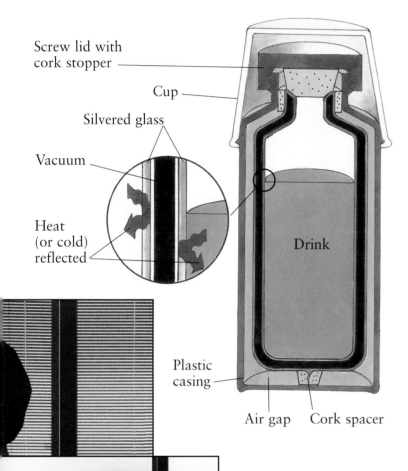

Screw lid with cork stopper

Cup

Silvered glass

Vacuum

Heat (or cold) reflected

Drink

Plastic casing

Air gap

Cork spacer

Tiny electronic parts can be put inside a sheet of glass. They change the way the particles of glass react to light. At the flick of a switch, the glass sheet in this office changes from a window to a wall.

MIRROR GLASS

The shiny, smooth surface of glass reflects, or throws back, some light, like a mirror. A real mirror has a glass front with a layer of flat, shiny metallic material behind it to reflect nearly all the light. Shiny glass and mirrors are also good at reflecting heat. In addition, glass is a good thermal insulator — it prevents the flow of heat. So glass is excellent for keeping warmth in (or out).

FACTS FROM THE PAST

Clear glass lets bright, warm sunshine through. But churches are usually meant to be cool and dim. So people made church windows of stained, or tinted, glass. Eventually, people decorated stained glass with pictures.

A religious scene on stained glass

SAFETY GLASS

Slivers of broken glass can be sharp and dangerous. Glass can be made safer and less likely to shatter when it is specially manufactured and treated.

STRONG GLASS

A sudden knock or hit is called an impact. Many plastics are impact-resistant. They bend when hit, but they do not shatter. This is because plastics are made of long, tiny molecules, which make them flexible. Since ordinary glass has no special tiny shapes or structures inside (*see page 6*), it is stiff and brittle. If hit, it does not bend — it breaks. It splits and shatters into countless sharp splinters. As shown on these pages, however, glass can be made stronger, tougher, and more impact-resistant.

Most types of glass crack and shatter into small, sharp pieces when they are hit.

Toughened, impact-resistant glass laminates are used for high-speed vehicles such as cars, trains, planes, and motorboats.

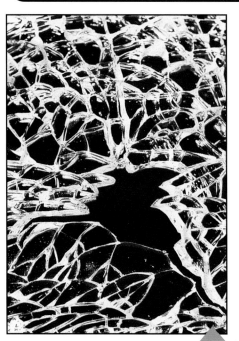

Closeup of a car's laminated windshield, which has cracked, but not shattered.

GLASS AND PLASTIC

Laminated glass is like a sandwich. Sheets of glass are stuck to a clear plastic sheet with see-through glue. This gives glass extra bending strength. If the glass cracks, the glue and plastic hold it together.

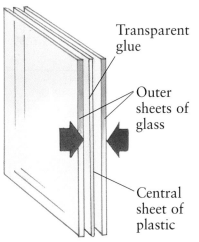

Transparent glue

Outer sheets of glass

Central sheet of plastic

GLASS PLUS

Various kinds of layers can be added to glass, such as clear plastic sheets, plastic nets, or metal mesh. Dipping glass in powerful chemicals, such as molten potassium salt, also makes it stronger. Another method, called thermal toughening, is shown on the next page.

IDEAS FOR THE FUTURE

Glass is clear and very hard, but not flexible. Plastics like acrylic are clear and bendable, but not very hard. Perhaps a new invention will be "Flexiglass." Then glass windows, covers, and domes could be folded up!

Unfolding a glass window

GLASS AND WIRE MESH

Long, ribbonlike sheets of glass are heated until soft and bendable. One sheet is fed through rollers, and strong wire mesh is pressed into it. Then another sheet of soft glass is pressed on top to make one sheet of glass with mesh inside. Even if the glass cracks, the wire mesh holds the pieces together. This type of glass is often used for protection and security.

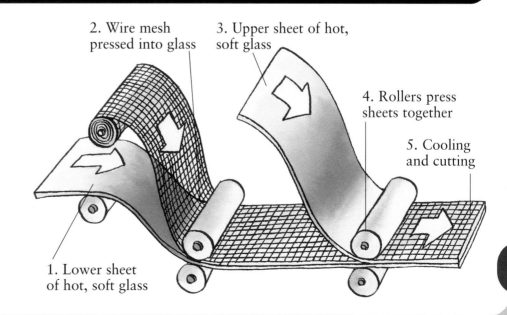

2. Wire mesh pressed into glass

3. Upper sheet of hot, soft glass

4. Rollers press sheets together

5. Cooling and cutting

1. Lower sheet of hot, soft glass

21

HEAT-RESISTANT GLASS

Ordinary glass begins to soften when heated to about 1,290° F (700° C). But some glass can withstand the higher temperatures of flames, fires, and furnaces.

"BORO" GLASS

Heat-resistant glass, like ordinary glass, is made mainly of silica (SiO_2). But about one-tenth of it is the chemical boric oxide (B_2O_3). Because of this, it is called borosilicate glass.

THERMAL TOUGHENING

Glass can be strengthened by heating it and then cooling its surfaces very quickly with jets of cold air. The result is a "sandwich" with two layers of fast-cooled glass on the outside and a slow-cooled layer between them. The middle layer toughens the outer layers by putting pressure on them. Thermal toughening works best on simply shaped pieces of glass, like flat or curved sheets and bowls.

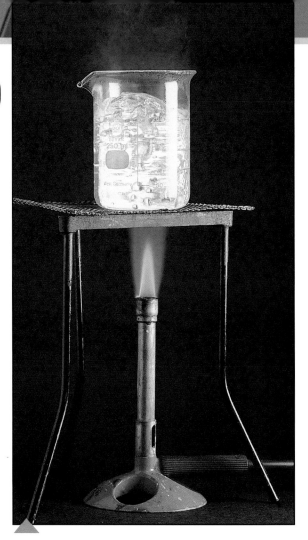

In the chemistry laboratory, glass beakers and flasks must be able to stand the heat of very hot flames.

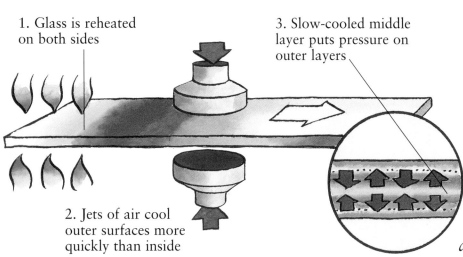

1. Glass is reheated on both sides

2. Jets of air cool outer surfaces more quickly than inside

3. Slow-cooled middle layer puts pressure on outer layers

Laboratory glassware is shaped and finished before it is toughened.

Because bright lights can get very hot, heat-resistant glass is used for floodlights in stadiums and theaters and for bright headlights on cars and trucks.

HEAT AND LIGHT

Borosilicate glass does not start to soften until it is hotter than 1,470° F (800° C) and does not melt until about 2,370° F (1,300° C) or above. This makes it very useful where temperatures are high — not only near furnaces and flames, but also in cookers and ovens. Ovenproof and flameproof glass dishes, bowls, and saucepans are usually made from this type of glass. Another important use for borosilicate glass is in very bright, high-power lights. But borosilicate glass is more costly than ordinary glass. This is because its raw materials are more expensive, and they must be heated to greater temperatures in the furnace when the molten glass is made.

PYREX
PERMET DE SURVEILLER
A TOUT INSTANT LA CUISSON
PARCEOU'IL EST
TRANSPARENT

See what's cooking!

FACTS FROM THE PAST

The first main heat-resistant glass was invented in 1915 by the Corning Glass Works. It was given the brand name Pyrex. Pyrex glass makes great cooking dishes because, unlike metal and ceramic, it lets you see if your food is burning without taking off the lid!

23

GLASS FIBERS AND WOOL

As we have seen, most glass is stiff. If you try to bend it, it snaps. But you can tie glass fibers in knots!

"HAIRS" OF GLASS

If glass is made in the form of long, narrow strings, or fibers, then it is more flexible, or bendable. Glass fibers can be made thinner than human hairs. They can be produced as separate strands, or they can be matted together like wool.

Blasts of hot air make glass fibers shoot out longer and thinner.

GLASS WOOL OR FIBERGLASS

Like most glass products, glass wool begins as molten glass. It flows into a spinning dish called a crown, with many tiny holes around its edge, shoots through the holes, and quickly hardens into thin fibers. A bonding chemical is added to stick the fibers together into a loose mat. The mat is then trimmed along the edges, cut into lengths, and rolled up.

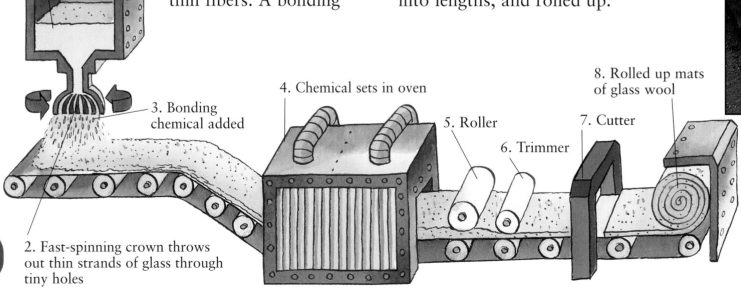

1. Molten glass

2. Fast-spinning crown throws out thin strands of glass through tiny holes

3. Bonding chemical added

4. Chemical sets in oven

5. Roller

6. Trimmer

7. Cutter

8. Rolled up mats of glass wool

KEEP THE HEAT

Glass itself is a good insulator. One major use for glass fibers is home insulation made of glass wool or fiberglass, which keeps heat in (or out). A layer or blanket of glass fibers traps air, and trapped air is also a good insulator. Glass fibers also last for a very long time. Unlike natural fibers, such as wool or cotton, glass fibers do not rot away or become moldy if it gets damp.

GLASS AND PLASTIC

Glass fibers are also put into glass-reinforced plastic, or GRP. The fibers give strength and stiffness, while the plastic bends to cope with shocks. GRP is impact-resistant, and it can be molded into the shapes of items such as "hardhat" helmets, boat hulls, and car bodies.

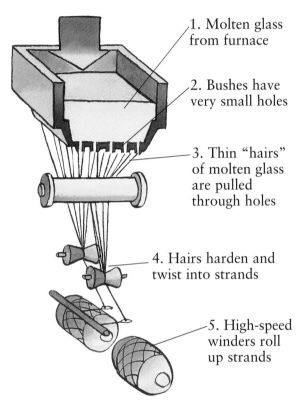

Very long, hairlike fibers of glass are formed by pulling molten glass through tiny holes in metal shapes called bushes. The fibers come together into bundles called strands, which are like thin ropes of glass. These strands are used to strengthen or reinforce plastic and even cement.

1. Molten glass from furnace

2. Bushes have very small holes

3. Thin "hairs" of molten glass are pulled through holes

4. Hairs harden and twist into strands

5. High-speed winders roll up strands

Glass wool or fiberglass is ideal for insulation in roofs, walls, and floors. It keeps heat in and cold out and does not rot or catch fire. It also keeps out noise.

IDEAS FOR THE FUTURE

Warm thermal clothing is made of fibers that are woven into layers. One day, glass fibers may be used to make clothing. They might work like glass in a greenhouse to reflect and keep in body heat. Of course, they would have to be made safe for skin!

Glass-fiber clothing would be ideal for mountain climbers.

OPTICAL GLASS

Optical glass is specially made to be as clear as possible. It is used to make eyeglasses, telescopes, cameras, and fiberoptic cables.

SEE THE LIGHT

The scientific study of light is called optics. Optics studies how glass reflects, or bounces, light; how it refracts, or bends, light; and how it splits light into different colors.

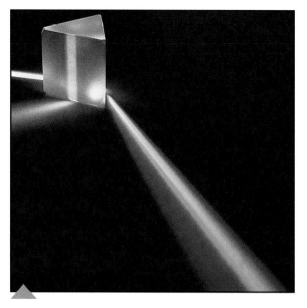

"White" light is really a mix of all the colors of the rainbow. A triangle-shaped glass prism bends light by different amounts and separates out the colors.

OPTICAL FIBERS

Each optical fiber is thinner than a human hair. It consists of a long, flexible rod made of two types of special glass, one inside the other. The fiber is formed by pulling molten glass through two tiny holes (*opposite*). Flashes of light pass along the core, or inner layer. When they hit the glass of the cladding, or outer layer, they reflect back. In this way, the light zigzags along the core.

Optical fibers are grouped into bundles called cables.

Light zigzags along core of optical fiber

This furnace heats glass until it just melts and then spins it so the glass spreads out into a large, curved mirror — the kind used in a giant telescope.

CRYSTAL CLEAR

Optical glass is used to make curved lenses, angular prisms, mirrors, and other items that alter light. It must be very clear so that light passes through it perfectly, without changing or distorting the light rays in any unwanted ways.

FLASHING FIBERS

Optical fibers carry flashes of laser light. These flashes are codes for information, such as the sounds of voices on telephone calls, cable TV programs, or e-mail messages. The fibers work faster and carry more signals than electrical signals passing along metal wires.

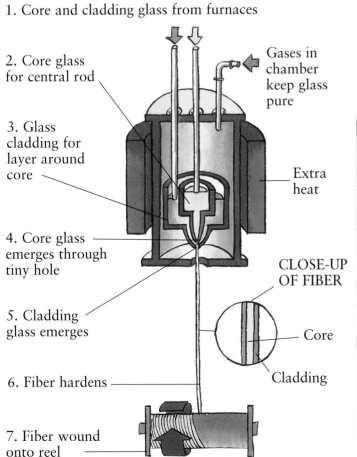

1. Core and cladding glass from furnaces

2. Core glass for central rod

3. Glass cladding for layer around core

Gases in chamber keep glass pure

Extra heat

4. Core glass emerges through tiny hole

5. Cladding glass emerges

CLOSE-UP OF FIBER

Core

Cladding

6. Fiber hardens

7. Fiber wound onto reel

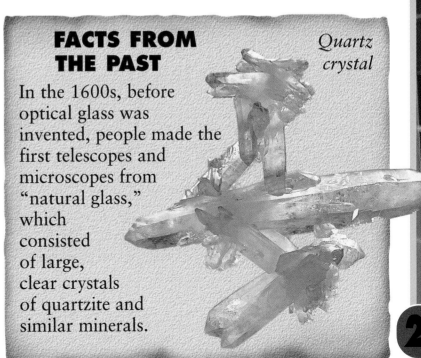

FACTS FROM THE PAST

Quartz crystal

In the 1600s, before optical glass was invented, people made the first telescopes and microscopes from "natural glass," which consisted of large, clear crystals of quartzite and similar minerals.

GLASS FOR THE FUTURE

Glass is made mainly from silica — sand. On the beach or in the desert, supplies of sand seem endless. So can we go on throwing away old glass and making new glass forever?

USE AGAIN

The raw materials for making glass include many other minerals and chemicals, some of which are very costly. Also, glassmaking furnaces and other equipment use huge amounts of energy, especially heat. This is why it is very important for us to reuse glass items like bottles and jars instead of always buying new ones.

Recycling glass uses one-third less energy than making new glass, and it cuts down on the need for raw materials by three-quarters.

One of the first great glass buildings was the Crystal Palace in London, England. It was finished in 1851. Intended to last for centuries, it was destroyed by fire in 1936.

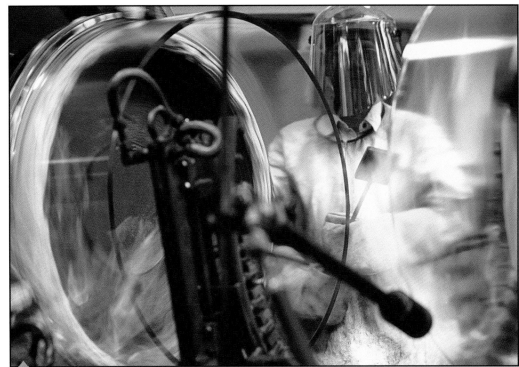

Skill and craftsmanship are needed for making specialized glassware.

RECYCLING GLASS

Glass is one of the easiest substances to recycle. Old, broken, and scrap glass — together known as cullet — are cleaned and crushed, then added to the furnace at the start of the glassmaking process. Nearly all cities collect used glass for recycling.

NEW KINDS OF GLASS

For centuries, people have invented new kinds of glass and new uses for it. This is certain to continue. From glass that is stronger than steel to windows that can change color or show pictures, glass will continue to be one of the world's most useful materials.

IDEAS FOR THE FUTURE

TV visors can show programs on tiny screens. New kinds of glass would make the pictures sharper, brighter, and more colorful. Visors might be used for computer screens, too.

TV — in your face!

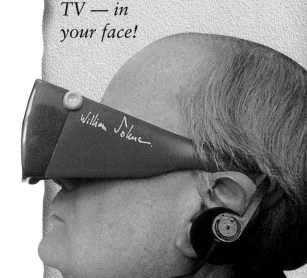

29

GLASS CHART

TYPE OF GLASS	QUALITIES AND USES
Soda-lime silica glass ("ordinary" glass)	Inexpensive, strong, easy to shape, easy to clean, and easy to recycle; used for bottles, jars, and everyday containers
Soda-lime silica glass with extra sodium	Relatively inexpensive, made by float process, resists weather, can be toughened; used for windowpanes and similar sheets
Soda-lime silica glass with yet more sodium	Fairly inexpensive, can be blown or shaped quickly from ribbons, clear, resists changes in temperature; used for light bulbs, fluorescent light tubes, and vacuum bottles
Soda-lime silica glass with extra magnesium and aluminum	Relatively inexpensive, tough, can withstand regular use, bright and clear, does not affect foods or drinks; used for drinking glasses, bowls, dishes, plates, and other everyday glassware
Soda-lime silica glass with extra minerals	Resists weather and temperature, easily pressed, strong; used for glass building blocks, walls, stairs, floors, roofs, partitions
Soda-lime silica glass with extra calcium and aluminum	Strong but light, resists chemicals, dampness, heat, and electricity, can be spun or drawn into very thin strands; used for glass fibers and wool, glass-reinforced plastic
Borosilicate glass (such as Pyrex)	Strong, easy to clean, resists chemicals, heat, microwaves; used for test tubes, laboratory equipment, ovenproof cookware
Lead glass (up to one-third lead oxide)	Heavy or dense, brilliant sparkling finish, can be shaped with great precision, can be engraved and patterned; used for "lead crystal" wineglasses and containers, handmade glass ornaments, decorations, and artworks
Lead glass — with added lead (up to two-thirds lead oxide)	Extremely heavy or dense, stops dangerous rays; used as shielding for protection against radioactivity in nuclear power stations and atomic research laboratories
Optical glass (varies greatly in raw materials)	Extremely clear, can be polished, resists temperature changes; used for cameras, eyeglasses, microscopes, binoculars, lasers, telescopes, and other devices that use light
Laminate glass (as a sandwich with plastic)	Very hard, strong, shatterproof; used for windshields, safety screens, and similar see-through protection from impacts

GLOSSARY

amorphous: shapeless; having no particular shape or structure.

anneal: to strengthen or toughen a substance by a careful combination of heating and cooling. The special oven-cooler used for this process is called an annealing lehr.

cullet: glass that is old, broken, or scrapped and can be used again in glassmaking.

draw: in glass shaping, to pull or stretch soft or molten glass so that it becomes longer and thinner.

impact: a knock, hit, bump, or similar physical shock.

molten: melted by heat into a liquid that can ooze and flow.

parison: a partly shaped lump of glass that will be fully shaped by blowing or molding to form the finished object.

pigment: a substance used to give color to another material, such as glass, paint, ink, or textiles.

reflect: to bounce back, as when sound waves bounce off a wall as an echo or light rays bounce off a mirror to form an image.

refract: to bend or change direction, as when light rays bend as they pass into or out of a glass object.

silica: a substance made of silicon and oxygen, like silicon dioxide (SiO_2), which is the main raw material for making glass.

MORE BOOKS TO READ

A Day in the Life of a Colonial Glassblower. The Library of Living and Working in Colonial Times series. J. L. Branse (Powerkids Press)

Fire into Ice: Adventures in Glass Making. James Houston (Tundra Books)

The Glassmakers. Colonial Craftsmen series. Leonard Everett Fisher (Benchmark Books)

WEB SITES

How Do You Recycle Glass?
http://www.consrv.ca.gov/dor/edu/howdoyou.htm

Corning Museum of Glass — Resources.
http://www.cmog.org/page.cfm?page=77

Due to the dynamic nature of the Internet, some web sites stay current longer than others. To find additional web sites, use a reliable search engine with one or more of the following keywords: *cullet, eyeglasses, fiberoptics, glass, glassblowing, insulation, Pyrex, recycling, sand, stained glass.*

INDEX